BELFAST CONFETTI

CIARAN CARSON

BELFAST CONFETTI

WAKE FOREST UNIVERSITY PRESS

Published in North America by Wake Forest University Press in December 1989. Text designed by Peter Fallon and published in Ireland by The Gallery Press, Loughcrew, Oldcastle, County Meath in November 1989.

ISBN-0-916390-40-3 (paper)
ISBN-0-916390-41-1 (cloth)

LC Card Number 89-040527

Contents

Acknowledgements

Some of these poems and essays were previously published in *The Irish Review*, *The Times Literary Supplement*, *The Honest Ulsterman*, *The London Review of Books*, *Gown* and *Rhinoceros*.

'Loaf' (under the title 'Sliced Pan Seventeen') won a Sotheby's Award in the 1987 Arvon/Observer International Poetry Competition.

'Bed-Time Story' and 'Ambition' appeared first in *The New Yorker*.

Many sources were consulted in the making of this book. I am especially grateful for Jonathan Bardon's very useful bibliography in his *Belfast: An Illustrated History* (Blackstaff Press). My versions of *haiku* are much indebted to Harold G. Henderson's marvellous anthology, *An Introduction to Haiku* (Doubleday Anchor Books, New York, 1958).

Do m'athair, Liam Mac Carráin

For my father, William Carson

PART ONE

Not to find one's way about in a city
is of little interest . . . But to lose one's
way in a city, as one loses one's way in
a forest, requires practice . . . I learned this
art late in life: it fulfilled the dreams
whose first traces were the labyrinths on
the blotters of my exercise books.

Walter Benjamin,
A Berlin Childhood Around
the Turn of the Century

Loaf

I chewed it over, this whiff I got just now, but trying to pin
down
That aroma - yeast, salt, flour, water – is like writing on the
waxed sleeve
That it's wrapped in: the nib keeps skidding off. Or the ink
won't take. Blue-black
Quink is what I used then. I liked the in-between-ness of it,
neither
One thing nor the other. A *Conway Stewart* fountain-pen,
blue-ish green
Mock tortoiseshell . . . the lever sticking sometimes in the quick
of my thumb,
I'd fill her up: a contented slurp like the bread you use to sup
up
Soup. McWatters' pan loaf, some said, was like blotting-paper:
I thought of
Leonardo's diary, or a mirror code ending with, *Eat this*.
Well, some people *like* blotting-paper. I used to eat chalk
myself. Raw
Flour, oatmeal. Paper. A vitamin deficiency? The corners of
My books weren't dog-eared, they were chewed. But neatly
chewed, like the thumb-index
Of a dictionary. I ate my way from *A* to *Z*, the list of weights
And measures. So now I'm in McWatters' flour-loft. Grains,
pecks and bushels:

So much raw material. *I* was raw. This was a summer job, not
real
Work. Myself and this other skiver, we mostly talked of this
and that –

Cigarettes and whiskey – between whatever it was we were supposed
To do. Joe reckoned that Jameson's *Three Swallows* was hard to beat
Though you could make a case for their *Robin Redbreast* or Power's *Gold Label*.
One had the edge the others didn't, though you couldn't quite describe it.
Like Gallaher's *Greens*: dry, smoky, biting. He had this bebop hairstyle –
Bee-bap, as they say in Belfast, a golden fuzz pricked up from the scalp –
And he'd done time at one time or another for some petty crime. Theft?
Jiggery-pokery. Night-shifts. The kind of fly moves that get you caught.
And as it happened, he was between times just then, like me between terms.

It seemed the Health Inspectors were due in a while, so we were given
Galvanized buckets, sponges, those mops with the head of an albino
Golliwog. The place breathed gunge and grease, the steamy damp of baking bread.
So as I say, we talked: football, drink, girls, horses, though I didn't know
Much on any of these scores. They were clouds on the blue of the future.
Walking the slippery catwalk from one bake-room to the next – like Dante's
Inferno, the midnight glare of ovens, a repeated doughy slap
Of moulds being filled – we'd think of the cool of the loo or a lunchtime pint.

The bitter edge of Guinness would cut through the bread and
　　oxtail soup
Till bread and soup and stout became all one. We would talk
　　with our mouths full.

Then back to *Ajax* and *Domestos*, the Augean pandemonium.
Or sorting out spoiled loaves for pig-feed – waxed wrappers in
　　one bag, sliced pan
In the other; the pigs, it seemed, were particular. At other
　　times,
Stacking up empty flour-sacks: cloudy caesurae floating one on
　　top
Of one another, the print so faded we could barely read the text;
That choked-up weave meant nothing much but passing time.
　　Expanding moments,
Watching dough rise, the stretch-marks lost in the enormous
　　puff-ball – *Is this*
The snow that was so bright last year?
　　　　　　　　　　　　　　　We worked slowly through
　　the levels, till
We found ourselves at last in No. 2 loft, high above the racket.
My last week. As for him, he didn't know. Muffled by forgotten
　　drifts
Of flour, I was thinking of the future, he was buried in the past.
This move he'd worked, this girl he'd known. Everything stored
　　away in cells.
Pent-up honey talk oozed out of him, while I sang, *Que sera sera.*

He asked if I'd remember him. We wrote our names on the
　　snowed-up panes.
The date, the names of girls, hearts and arrows. We made up
　　affairs between
The bakers and the packers – bread and paper – then we wiped
　　it all clean.

17

The glass shone for the first time in years. We were staring out
the window
At the end of summer. Aeroplanes flew by at intervals, going
elsewhere:
Tiny specks, the white lines of their past already fuzzing up the
blue.

Plains and mountains, skies
all up to their eyes in snow:
nothing to be seen.

    — Joso

Snow

A white dot flicked back and forth across the bay window: not
A table-tennis ball, but 'ping-pong', since this is happening in
   another era,
The extended leaves of the dining-table – scratched mahogany
   veneer –
Suggesting many such encounters, or time passing: the
   celluloid diminuendo
As it bounces off into a corner and ticks to an incorrigible
   stop.
I pick it up days later, trying to get that pallor right: it's neither
   ivory
Nor milk. Chalk is better; and there's a hint of pearl,
   translucent
Lurking just behind opaque. I broke open the husk so many
   times
And always found it empty; the pith was a wordless bubble.

Though there's nothing in the thing itself, bits of it come back
   unbidden,
Playing in the archaic dusk till the white blip became invisible.
Just as, the other day, I felt the tacky pimples of a ping-pong
   bat
When the bank-clerk counted out my money with her rubber
   thimble, and knew
The black was bleeding into red. Her face was snow and roses
   just behind
The bullet-proof glass: I couldn't touch her if I tried. I
   crumpled up the chit –
No use in keeping what you haven't got – and took a stroll
   to Ross's auction.

There was this Thirties scuffed leather sofa I wanted to make a
  bid for.
Gestures, prices: soundlessly collateral in the murmuring
  room.

I won't say what I paid for it: anything's too much when you
  have nothing.
But in the dark recesses underneath the cushions I found
  myself kneeling
As decades of the Rosary dragged by, the slack of years ago
  hauled up
Bead by bead; and with them, all the haberdashery of loss –
  cuff buttons,
Broken ball-point pens and fluff, old pennies, pins and
  needles, and yes,
A ping-pong ball. I cupped it in my hands like a crystal, seeing
  not
The future, but a shadowed parlour just before the blinds are
  drawn. Someone
Has put up two trestles. Handshakes all round, nods and
  whispers.
Roses are brought in, and suddenly, white confetti seethes
  against the window.

As a scarecrow blows
over: the first whispering
of the autumn wind.

— Kyoruku

All the Better to See You With

No soft pink or peach scheme for Rose-Marie O'Hara when
    she married:
Since her favourite colour was red, she was determined on a
    vivid red theme –
The bridesmaids were in scarlet lace and satin, armed with
    bouquets
Of vermilion roses; the friend's 'black taxi' which they
    borrowed for the bridal car
Was crimson lake. Into which they'd dive before the day was
    out. The invitations
Were, of course, red letters. My hands were shaking as I slit
    the envelope
And glimpsed the copperplate. My name. His and hers. All
    brought together
In a florid moment, a dashed-off sketch of what would happen,
    like this fox
I caught once in the corner of my eye, disappearing in a
    brambly thicket, its elongated brush
Hovering for an instant like a brush-stroke;
The kind of random mark that might be usefully retained for
    just that air
Of neither-here-nor-thereness. Coming in the act of going.

Some might have swamped the canvas in this red extravaganza,
    but convention
Was deferred to in her own ensemble: ivory organza, a tiered
    affair
With ruched bodice and hooped skirts, millefeuilles petticoats,
    and underneath

The trailing hem, if you could only lift it, red stilettos –
Such pretty shoes for dancing in, I don't think – which were, it
   seemed,
A bit too tight for comfort. Teetering up the knife-edge of the
   aisle,
Did she even then regret this? Whispers ran around her and
   jostled her dress.
Which she'd discard before the day was out.

Now the soles of the groom's feet are presented to me, hers are
   hidden
Still. She might have stepped into a muddied pool up to her
   ankles,
Or they are deep in the lacy avalanche. Thinking of *her cheeks like
   roses*
Or like blood dropped on snow, I would have climbed the
   Matterhorn for her,
Stood on my head, or run like a fox before hounds – through
   the copper beeches,
Glowing, bursting into thickets like the last coal stirred in the
   fire
Of his red hair. I'd blow and blow and try to stir it up again.
   Though still
I couldn't quite believe it. Like the wrong-sized foot
Stuck into this glass slipper, she was the glass and he was the
   foot.
Her own feet, lopped off, waltzed away into the forest.
How could I unravel all those brambles, tangles, nettles,
   thorns? I pulled
At jagged things, and more kept coming up in that erratic spiky
   hand
Of hers. Billets-doux, excuses, lies. Or a line or two that gave
   some hope . . .

I'd twist it inside out, this coil that led me on and on, and
    brings me back
To the red bud of his buttonhole, a shower of red confetti.

Or to this scenario of her as Wolf, and me as Little Red Riding
    Hood
Being gobbled up. *Many's the strawberry grows in the salt sea*, as
    the song
Would have it, *and many's the ship sails in the forest*: it's time for
    the fox
To go to earth. I painted a picture of myself curled up, the
    brush
Like a knife between my teeth. A few careless dribbles,
    incarnadine upon my wrist.
The newly-weds were found in a wood. His face was
    pockmarked by a fever
Of stilettos. Her belly was unstitched. Tomato ketchup
    flicked on her portrait.
Everything dissolves: the white spirit clouds with rust and
    cinnabar.

I know the wild geese
ate my barley – yesterday?
Today? Where did they go?

— Yasui

Ambition

> *'I did not allow myself to think of ultimate escape . . .
> one step at a time was enough.'*
> John Buchan, *Mr Standfast*

Now I've climbed this far, it's time to look back. But smoke
  obscures
The panorama from the Mountain Loney spring. The city and
  the mountain are on fire.
My mouth's still stinging from the cold sharp shock of water –
  a winter taste
In summer – but my father's wandered off somewhere. I can't
  seem to find him.
We'd been smoking 'coffin nails', and he'd been talking of his
  time inside, how
Matches were that scarce, you'd have to split them four ways
  with your thumb-nail;
And seven cigarette ends made a cigarette. *Keep a thing for
  seven years,*
You'll always find a use for it, he follows in the same breath . . . it
  reminds me
Of the saint who, when he had his head cut off, picked up his
  head, and walked
With it for seven miles. And the wise man said, *The distance
  doesn't matter,*
It's the first step that was difficult.

Any journey's like that – *the first step of your life,* my father
  interrupts –
Though often you take one step forward, two steps back. For if
  time is a road,
It's fraught with ramps and dog-legs, switchbacks and
  spaghetti; here and there,

27

The dual carriageway becomes a one-track, backward mind.
   And bits of the landscape
Keep recurring: it seems as if I've watched the same suburban
   tennis match
For hours, and heard, at ever less-surprising intervals, the
   applause of pigeons
Bursting from a loft. Or the issue is not yet decided, as the
   desultory handclaps
Turn to rain. The window that my nose is pressed against is
   breathed-on, giving
Everything a sfumato air. I keep drawing faces on it, or prac-
   tising my signature.

And if time is a road, then you're checked again and again
By a mobile checkpoint. One soldier holds a gun to your head.
   Another soldier
Asks you questions, and another checks the information on the
   head computer.
Your name. Your brothers' names. Your father's name. His
   occupation. As if
The one they're looking for is not you, but it might be you.
   Looks like you
Or smells like you. And suddenly, the posthumous aroma of an
   empty canvas
Postman's sack – twine, ink, dead letters – wafts out from the
   soldiers'
Sodden khaki. It's obvious they're bored: one of them is watch-
   ing Wimbledon
On one of those postage-stamp-sized TV screens. *Of course, the
   proper shot,*
An unseen talking head intones, *should have been the lob.* He's
   using words like
Angled, volley, smash and *strategy.* Someone is *fighting a losing
   battle.*

Isn't that the way, that someone tells you what you should have done, when
  You've just done the opposite? *Did you give the orders for this man's death?*
On the contrary, the accused replies, as if he'd ordered birth or resurrection.
Though *one nail drives out another*, as my father says.

And my father should have known better than to tamper with Her Majesty's
Royal Mail – or was it His, then? His humour was to take an Irish ha'penny
With the harp on the flip side, and frank a letter with it. Some people didn't
See the joke; they'd always thought him a Republican. He was reported,
Laid off for a month. Which is why he never got promoted. So one story goes.
The other is a war-time one, where he's supposed to go to England
For a training course, but doesn't, seeing he doesn't want to get conscripted.
My mother's version is, he lacked ambition. He was too content to stay
In one place. He liked things as they were . . . *perfect touch, perfect timing, perfect*
Accuracy: the commentary has just nudged me back a little, as I manage
To take in the action replay. There's a tiny puff of chalk, as the ball skids off
The line, like someone might be firing in slow motion, far away: that otherwise
Unnoticeable faint cloud on the summer blue, which makes the sky around it

All the more intense and fragile.

It's nearer to a winter blue. A zig-zag track of footsteps is imprinted
On the frosted tennis-court: it looks as if the Disappeared One rose before
First light, and stalked from one side of the wire cage to the other, off
Into the glinting laurels. No armed wing has yet proclaimed responsibility:
One hand washes the other, says my father, as sure as *one funeral makes many*.
For the present is a tit-for-tat campaign, exchanging *now* for *then*,
The Christmas post of Christmas Past, the black armband of the temporary man;
The insignia have mourned already for this casual preserve. Threading
Through the early morning suburbs and the monkey-puzzle trees, a smell of coffee lingers,
Imprisoned in the air like wisps of orange peel in marmalade; and sleigh-bell music
Tinkles on the radio, like ice cubes in a summer drink. I think I'm starting, now,
To know the street map with my feet, just like my father.

God never shuts one door, said my father, *but he opens up another*; and then,
I walked the iron catwalk naked in the freezing cold: he's back into his time
As internee, the humiliation of the weekly bath. It was seven weeks before
He was released: it was his younger brother they were after all the time.

God never opens one door, but he shuts another: my uncle was inside
   for seven years.
At his funeral, they said how much I looked like him: I've got
   his smoker's cough,
At any rate. And now my father's told to cut down on the
   cigarettes, he smokes
Them three or four puffs at a time. Stubs them out and lights
   them, seven times.
I found him yesterday a hundred yards ahead of me, struggling,
   as the blazing
Summer hauled him one step at a time into a freezing furnace.
   And with each step
He aged. As I closed in on him, he coughed. I coughed. He
   stopped and turned,
Made two steps back towards me, and I took one step forward.

To Lord Toba's hall
five or six horsemen blow in:
storm-wind of the fall.

— Buson

Queen's Gambit

A Remote Handling Equipment (Tracked) Explosive
  Ordnance Disposal unit – *Wheelbarrow*,
For short – is whirring and ticking towards the Ford Sierra
  parked in Tomb Street,

Its robotic arm extended indirectly towards this close-up of a
  soldier. He's wearing
An M69 flak jacket, Dr Marten boots and non-regulation
  skiing gloves.

Another soldier, armed with Self-loading Rifle, squats
  beneath a spray-gunned
Flourish of graffiti: *The Provos Are Fighting For You. Remember
It. Brits Out.*

Now they're seen together leaning against the façade of a
  chemist's shop,
Admiring – so it would appear – the cardboard ad. for
  Wilkinson Sword razor blades.

So much, they're now in the interior: a gauzy, pinkish smell of
  soap and sticking-
Plaster, through which they spit word-bubbles at the white-
  coated girl assistant.

Much of this is unintelligible, blotted out by stars and
  asterisks
Just as the street outside is splattered with bits of corrugated
  iron and confetti.

Her slightly antiseptic perfume is a reminiscent *je-ne-sais-quoi*
Glimpsed through Pear's Soap, an orange-sepia zest of
    coal-tar –

It's that moiré light from the bathroom window, or a body
    seen behind
The shower-curtain, holding a Champagne telephone – the
    colour, not the drink,

Though it gives off a perceptible hiss. And the continuous
    background
Rumble is a string of *M*s and *R*s, expanding and contracting

To reveal the windswept starry night, through which a
    helicopter trawls
Its searchlight. Out there, on the ground, there's a spoor of
    Army boots;

Dogs are following their noses, and terrorists are contemplating
Terror, a glittering, tilted view of mercury, while the
    assistant slithers

Into something more comfortable: jeans, a combat jacket, Doc
    Marten boots;
Then weighs the confidential dumb-bell of the telephone. She
    pushes buttons:

Zero Eight Double Zero. Then the number of the Beast, the
    number of the Beast
Turned upside down: Six Six Six, Nine Nine Nine . . .

The ambient light of yesterday is amplified by talk of might-
    have-beens,
Making 69 – the year – look like quotation marks, comment-
    ators commentating on

The flash-point of the current Trouble, though there's any
    God's amount
Of Nines and Sixes: 1916, 1690, The Nine Hundred Years'
    War, whatever.

Or maybe we can go back to the Year Dot, the nebulous
    expanding brain-wave
Of the Big Bang, releasing us and It and everything into
    oblivion;

It's so hard to remember, and so easy to forget the casualty list –
Like the names on a school desk, carved into one another till
    they're indecipherable.

It's that frottage effect again: the paper that you're scribbling
    on is grained
And blackened, till the pencil-lead snaps off, in a valley of the
    broken alphabet

And the streets are a bad photostat grey: the ink comes off on
    your hand.
With so many foldings and unfoldings, whole segments of the
    map have fallen off.

It's not unlike the missing reel in the film, the blank screen
    jittering
With numerals and flak, till the picture jumps back – a bit out
    of sync,

35

As soldiers A and B and others of the lettered regiment discuss
    the mission
In their disembodied voices. Only the crackly Pye Pocketfone
    sounds real,

A bee-in-the-biscuit-tin buzzing number codes and decibels.
    They're in the belly
Of a Saracen called 'Felix', the cartoon cat they've taken as a
    mascot:

It's all the go, here, changing something into something else,
    like rhyming
Kampuchea with Cambodia. It's why Mickey Mouse wears
    those little white gloves –

Claws are too much like a mouse. And if the animals are trying
    to be people,
Vice versa is the case as well. Take 'Mad Dog' Reilly, for
    example, who

This instant is proceeding to the rendezvous. A gunman, he
    isn't yet; the rod
Is stashed elsewhere, somewhere in a mental block of dog-leg
    turns and cul-de-sacs.

He sniffs his hand, an antiseptic tang that momentarily brings
    back
The creak of a starched coat crushed against his double-
    breasted gaberdine.

After the recorded message, the bleep announces a magnetic
    silence

Towards which she's drawn as conspirator, as towards a
    confessional, whispering

What she knows into the wire-grilled darkness: names, dates,
    places;
More especially, a future venue, Tomb Street GPO.

She wants the slate wiped clean, *Flash* or *Ajax* cutting a bright
    swathe
Through a murky kitchen floor, transforming it into a gleaming
    checkerboard.

Tiles of black and white on which the regiments of pawns move
    ponderously,
Bishops take diagonals, and the Queen sees dazzling lines
    of power.

Or, putting it another way, Operation 'Mad Dog', as it's known
    now,
Is the sketch that's taking shape on the Army HQ blackboard,
    chalky ghosts

Behind the present, showing what was contemplated and
    rubbed out, Plan A
Becoming X or Y; interlocked, curved arrows of the mortgaged
    future.

The raffia waste-paper bin is full of crumpled drafts and
    cigarette butts,
And ash has seeped through to the carpet. There's a smell of
    peeled oranges.

But the Unknown Factor, somewhat like the Unknown Soldier,
    has yet to take

37

The witness box. As someone spills a cup of tea on a discarded
    Irish News

A minor item bleeds through from another page, blurring
    the main story.
It's difficult to pick up without the whole thing coming apart
    in your hands,

But basically it invokes this bunch of cowboys, who,
    unbeknownst to us all,
Have jumped on board a Ford Sierra, bound for You-Know-
    Where.

They're Ordinary Criminals: you know them by the dollar
    signs that shiver
In their eyes, a notion that they're going to hit the jackpot
    of the GPO.

Unbeknownst to themselves, they'll be picked up in the
    amplified light
Of a Telescope Starlight II Night Observation Device
    (NOD) – *Noddy*, for short,

But not before the stoolie-pigeon spool is reeled back;
    amplified,
Its querulous troughs and peaks map out a different curve of
    probability.

My newly-lowered ears in the barber's mirror were starting to
    take on a furtive look.
A prison cut – my face seemed Born Again – but then, I'd asked
    for *short*.

And I've this problem, talking to a man whose mouth is a
    reflection.
I tend to think the words will come out backwards, so I'm
    saying nothing.

And then, says he, – he's staring straight into my eyes, the
    scissors poised –
It seems they think they're just about to nail your man O'Reilly

*When a bunch of hoods pulls up in a Ford Sierra and jumps out with the
    sawn-off*
*Shotguns, plastic masks they must have got in Elliot's – Mickey Mouse,
    Donald Duck*

*And Pluto – too much watching TV, if you ask me – so of course the
    Brits let go*
With everything. He snips at my right ear. *But now hear this:*

*This Post Office van bombs out from Tomb Street loading bay, its side
    door open*
And they've got this effing Gatling gun or something going full blast –

*Dot, dot, dot, dot – and the Brits are all shot up – could you move your
    head a bit –*
*Right – so the Mad Dog, he jumps in the back and him and the boys are off
    like a shot.*

*So what do you think? It looks to me, it was a set-up job, though who
    exactly*
*Was set up, God only knows. You can see it for yourself – they've been
    checking out*

*That Ford Sierra for the past two hours, just as soon as it was
    light.*

39

Seems they think the Disney characters were in on it. If you ask
   me,
With these confidential telephones, you never know who's doing who, or
   why.
Better to keep your mouth shut, that's what I say. Haircut OK, sir?

He held a mirror to my neck. I nodded. He shook out the cloth,
   and curls
And snippets writhed like commas on the chessboard tiles.
   Now that I could see

Myself without the hair and beard, I looked like someone else.
   He brushed
My shoulders, and I left him to a row of empty mirrors, sweep-
   ing up

The fallen swathes. Turning into Tomb Street, I began to feel a
   new man.
Perfume breathed from somewhere, opening avenues of love, or
   something déjà vu.

These are wild slow days,
echoes trickling in from all
around Kyoto.

— Buson

PART TWO

. . . that the Mastive dogs belonginge to Butchers,
Tanners, and other Inhabitants dwelling in this
Corporation and the suburbs and ffields thereunto
belonginge, have Barbarously ffallen upon horses
in Carrs, upon the Street, and also horses out of
carrs, And have violently Torne and abused them,
That some of them have been in hazard to die, And
also ffallen upon severall cattell bothe upon the
Streets and in the ffields. Inso much that severall
catell are mightily abused, and some of them killed
to the great loss of many of the poore Inhabitants
of this Corporacon. And also that the said Dogs
have ffallen upon severall men and boyes upon the
Streets and Lanes of this Towne and suburbs
thereunto belonginge, and have pult them to the
Ground, Torne their cloathes and Torne some of their
ffleshe and eaten the same Insoemuch that many
Inhabitants ffeare their lives to walk the streets
or laines either by night or day for the said
dogs and Bitches . . .

Ordinance of the Corporation of Belfast,
25th July 1678

Gate

Passing *Terminus* boutique the other day, I see it's got a bit of
    flak:
The *T* and the *r* are missing, leaving *e minus*, and a sign saying,
    MONSTER
CLOSING DOWN SALE. It opened about six months back, selling
    odd-job-lots,
Ends of ranges. Before that it was Burton's, where I bought my
    wedding suit.
Which I only wear for funerals, now. *Gone for a Burton*, as the
    saying goes.

The stopped clock of *The Belfast Telegraph* seems to indicate the
    time
Of the explosion – or was that last week's? Difficult to keep
    track:
Everything's a bit askew, like the twisted pickets of the
    security gate, the wreaths
That approximate the spot where I'm told the night patrol
    went through.

Last Orders

Squeeze the buzzer on the steel mesh gate like a trigger, but
It's someone else who has you in their sights. Click. It opens.
  Like electronic
Russian roulette, since you never know for sure who's who, or
  what
You're walking into. I, for instance, could be anybody. Though
  I'm told
Taig's written on my face. See me, would *I* trust appearances?

Inside a sudden lull. The barman lolls his head at us. We order
  Harp –
Seems safe enough, everybody drinks it. As someone looks
  daggers at us
From the *Bushmills* mirror, a penny drops: how simple it would
  be for someone
Like ourselves to walk in and blow the whole place, and
  ourselves, to Kingdom Come.

Farset

Trying to get back to that river, this river I am about to explore, I imagine or remember peering between the rusted iron bars that lined one side of the alleyway behind St Gall's School at the bottom of Waterville Street, gazing down at the dark exhausted water, my cheeks pressed against the cold iron. It is only years later I will find its name. For now I take it in with a child's rapt boredom. Muck. Water. A bottomless bucket. The undercarriage of a pram. A rusted spring mattress. The river, the stream, the sewer trickles from a black mouth and disappears down a black hole. It is this which gives Belfast its name.

> *The utmost obscurity and perplexity, however, attend the derivation of the name . . . the name of* Bealafarsad, *which means, according to some, hurdleford town, while others have translated it, the mouth of the pool. Either of these explanations might receive some corroboration from local facts, but as it is a matter of complete hypothesis, there seems to be further room for further speculation.*

So says George Benn, writing in the 1820s. Dubourdieu, writing some years earlier, claims that Belfast *is supposed to have derived its present name from Bela Fearsad, which signifies a town at the mouth of a river, expressive of the circumstances, in which it stood.* Ward, Lock & Co.'s *Guide to Northern Ireland*, a hundred-odd years later, has yet another version: *While the bell in Belfast's civic coat of arms is a feeble pun, the word 'fast' refers to the 'farset', or sandbank (also the now-covered-in High Street river). 'Bel' in Celtic means 'ford', i.e. Bel-feirste, the 'bel' or 'ford' of the 'farset'.*

In all this watery confusion one thing seems certain: that *Belfast* is a corruption of the Irish *Béal Feirste*. *Béal* is easy. It means a mouth, or the mouth of a river; an opening; an approach. Benn's informant seems to have mistaken it for *baile*, a town, thereby arriving at an English equivalent of the modern Irish name for Dublin, *Baile Átha Cliath*, which is precisely *hurdleford town*. But it is this *feirste* in which meaning founders, this genitive of *fearsad*, the Irish word for . . . .

The Rev. Dineen glosses it as a shaft; a spindle; the ulna of the arm; a club; the spindle of an axle; a bar or bank of sand at low water; a deep narrow channel on a strand at low tide; a pit or pool of water; a verse, a poem. The dictionaries of Edward O'Reilly and Thomas de Vere Conys agree substantially, though O'Reilly has the strange *wallet*, which turns up again in Duelly's Scottish Gaelic dictionary; and he has the nice adjective *fearsach, full of little ridges in the sand*, one of those illuminations glimpsed at dawn's low tide, where seeming *terra firma* mimics the ridges of the sea: I remember seeing this precisely in the remote Gaeltacht of *Rann na Feirste*, or Ranafast in Donegal. Not to mention *Béal Feirste*, or Belfarset in County Mayo, where I have never been.

But let us take the simple approach, and imagine that *fearsad* is a sandbank, formed by the confluence of the river of that name – the Farset – and the Lagan. So Belfast is the *approach to the sandbank*, or the *mouth of the Farset*; or the *approach to the ford*, since historically there was a ford at that point, and St George's Church in High Street, below which the Farset runs, reputedly stands on the site of the *Chapel by the Ford*. Or let us suppose, with the Jesuit McCionnaith's English-Irish dictionary, that *fearsad* stands for *axis*, as in the expression, *Bíonn an domhan ag casadh ar a fhearsaid féin, the world revolves on its own axis:* one

48

imagines this, not as a scientific observation, but as a stock response to another's elaborate and banal anecdote. And my father tells me that the Axis forces in the Second World War were indeed known as *Lucht na Feirste*, or the Axis People (not to be confused with the X People of the eponymous SF novel dreamed up by Belfast's ex-political-correspondent of the BBC, W. D. Flackes). Or more fancifully, we could take Dineen's *poem* and let Belfast be the *mouth of the poem* – surely Farset is related to the Latin turn in the furrow known as *versus*? And strangely, by a conspiracy of history and accident and geography, the river Farset, this hidden stream, is all these things: it is the axis of the opposed Catholic Falls Road and the Protestant Shankill, as we follow it through the old Shankill Graveyard – now a municipal park – till it disappears beneath the Shankill Road and surfaces in Bombay Street (burned down in the '68 Troubles), sidles along the back of Cupar Street, following almost precisely the line of the Peace-Line, this thirty-foot-high wall of graffiticized corrugated iron, the interface, the deadline, lost in what survives of Belfast's industrial Venice – for water, after all, was power – a maze of dams, reservoirs, sluices, sinks, footbridges that I remember in my dreams as walled-in by Titanic mills, gouts of steam breaking intermittently through the grit and smog, as it sinks and surfaces finally in Millfield and then is lost in its final culvert under High Street. It remembers spindles, arms, the songs of mill-girls. It remembers nothing: no one steps in the same river twice. Or, as some wag has it, no one steps in the same river once.

Hairline Crack

It could have been or might have been. Everything Provisional
    and Sticky,
Daily splits and splinters at the drop of a hat or a principle –
The right hand wouldn't even know it was the right hand; some
    would claim it
As the left. If only this, if only that, if only pigs could fly.
Someone decides, hawk or dove. Ambushes are sprung. Velvet
    fist. Iron glove.

It was on the stroke of midnight by the luminous dial of the
    clock
When this woman, caught in crossfire, stooped for the dash-
    board cigarette lighter.
In that instant, a bullet neatly parted her permanent wave. So
    now
She tells the story, how a cigarette made all the odds. Between
    life. And death.

Bloody Hand

Your man, says the Man, *will walk into the bar like this* – here his
    fingers
Mimic a pair of legs, one stiff at the knee – *so you'll know exactly*
What to do. He sticks a finger to his head. Pretend it's child's
    play –
The hand might be a horse's mouth, a rabbit or a dog. Five
    handclaps.
Walls have ears: the shadows you throw are the shadows you
    try to throw off.

I snuffed out the candle between finger and thumb. Was it the
    left hand
Hacked off at the wrist and thrown to the shores of Ulster?
    Did Ulster
Exist? Or the Right Hand of God, saying *Stop* to this and *No*
    to that?
My thumb is the hammer of a gun. The thumb goes up. The
    thumb goes down.

Schoolboys and Idlers of Pompeii

On an almost-blank wall where East 46th Street intersects Avenue A in the area called Alphabet City in New York, New York, is this graffito in three-foot-high black letters, saying BELFAST, with the cross-stroke of the T extended into an arrow pointing east, to Belfast. I have a photograph to prove this, but it's lost. In New York, no one that I ask seems to know the meaning of this careful scrawl, whether it's a gang, the code-word of a gang, a fashion, a club, or the name of the city where I was born; but the latter seems unlikely, though Alphabet City – barricaded liquor stores, secretive tobacco shops and elaborate Russian Orthodox churches – resembles Belfast, its roads pocked and skid-marked, littered with broken glass and crushed beer-cans.

And on the back wall of Gallaher's tobacco factory in North Queen Street in Belfast there has recently appeared this New York underground graffiti mural – coded, articulated, multi-coloured spray-gunned alphabet – pointing west by style and implication.

At times it seems that every inch of Belfast has been written-on, erased, and written-on again: messages, curses, political imperatives, but mostly names, or nicknames – Robbo, Mackers, Scoot, Fra – sometimes litanized obsessively on every brick of a gable wall, as high as the hand will reach, and sometimes higher, these snakes and ladders cancelling each other out in their bid to be remembered. *Remember 1690. Remember 1916.* Most of all, *Remember me. I was here.*

Remembering is one of the main functions of the Falls Road Club which meets on the first Thursday of every month in the Woolongong Bar in Adelaide, Australia. Exiled here since the emigrations of the Fifties and the early Sixties, these Kennedys and McErleans and Hugheses begin with small talk of the present, but are soon immersed in history, reconstructing a city on the other side of the world, detailing streets and shops and houses which for the most part only exist now in the memory. Or ghosts which exist only in the memory: someone is telling the story of the policeman who was shot dead outside the National Bank at the corner of Balaklava Street in 1922; but the story does not concern the policeman; rather, it is about the tin can which was heard that night rolling down Balaklava Street into Raglan Street, and which was heard again for years after, whenever there was trouble in the offing; thousands heard it, no one saw it. Someone else produces a week-old copy of *The Irish News* which gives another slant to the story: the tin can has not been heard since the streets concerned were demolished; this is hardly surprising, since even ghosts must have somewhere to live. Someone else again ventures the notion that the ghost is only a by-product of the elaborate version of hide-and-seek known as *kick-the-tin,* and they all start to remember more, their favourite hidey-holes in entries and alleyways and back yards, till they are lost in the comforting dusk and smog and drizzle of the Lower Falls, playing: games of imitation, games of chance, of luck, of initiation; the agglomerate tag or *tig* called *chain-tig.* Or they recall the names carved on the desks of Slate Street School, the taste of school milk in winter, the aura of plasticine and chalk-dust as they chant the twelve-times table for the twelfth or thirteenth time. Fortified by expensively-imported *Red Heart* Guinness and

Gallaher's *Blues*, they talk on, trying to get back – before the blitz, the avalanche, the troubles – the drinker interrupted between cup and lip – winding back the clock . . . .

The walls where they inscribed their names have been pulled down, but somewhere they survive. *Graffito*, says the dictionary, *a mural scribbling or drawing, as by schoolboys and idlers at Pompeii, Rome, and other ancient cities* . . . .

Running back the film of the mind's eye, the alphabet soup of demolition sorts itself into phrases, names, buildings, as if, on the last day, not only bodies are resurrected whole and perfect, but each brick, each stone, finds its proper place again:

the spire of St Malachy's Church, which was *removed, with advantage, for the tolling of the great bell in it interfered with the satisfactory maturing of the whiskey in Messrs. Dunville's adjacent distillery* . . .

the seven arches of the Long Bridge which fell in, *weakened by the passage of Schomberg's heavy cannon on their way to the Battle of the Boyne* . . .

the Great Salt Water Bridge, which still exists, *for it was not taken down when the Boyne Bridge was built, but was simply incorporated into the new structure and completely enveloped by it* . . .

bridges within bridges, the music in bad whiskey, the demolished air-raid shelters used as infill for the reclaimed land of Belfast Lough – who will sort out the chaos? Where does land begin, and water end? Or memory falter, and imagination take hold?

Barfly

Maybe you can figure it, why The Crown and Shamrock and
  The Rose and Crown
Are at opposite ends of the town. Politics? The odds change.
  The borders move.
Or they're asked to. A nod's as good as a wink. For example, in
  The Arkle Inn
This night, I'm getting it from the horse's mouth, when these
  two punters walk in,
Produce these rods, and punctuate the lunchtime menu:
  there's confetti everywhere.

Which, I take it, was a message. Or an audio-visual aid. At
  any rate, I buzzed off.
For, like the menu, everything's chalked up, and every now
  and then, wiped clean.
So now, I am a hyphen, flitting here and there: between The
  First and Last –
The Gamble – The Rendezvous – The Cellars – The Crow's
  Nest – The Elephant – The Fly.

Jump Leads

As the eggbeater spy in the sky flickered overhead, the TV
   developed a facial tic
Or as it turned out, the protesters had handcuffed them-
   selves to the studio lights.
Muffled off-camera, shouts of *No*. As I tried to lip-read the
   talking head
An arms cache came up, magazines laid out like a tray of
   wedding rings.
The bomb-disposal expert whose face was in shadow for
   security reasons

Had started very young by taking a torch apart at Christmas
   to see what made it tick.
Everything went dark. The killers escaped in a red Fiesta
   according to sources.
Talking, said the Bishop, is better than killing. Just before the
   Weather
The victim is his wedding photograph. He's been spattered
   with confetti.

Question Time

A native of Belfast, writes George Benn in his 1823 history of the city, *who had been brought up in one of the best streets which it contained, lately came over from America, after nearly a life-long absence, to visit the home of his youth. He could hardly find it. An immense place of business occupied its site, and he compared Belfast to an American town, so great was its progress in his absence, and so unexampled the growth of its population.*

That disorientation, that disappointed hunger for a familiar place, will be experienced all the more keenly by today's returning native; more than that, even the little piggy who stayed at home will sometimes feel lost. *I know this place like the back of my hand* – except who really knows how many hairs there are, how many freckles? A wound, a suture, and excision will remind us of the physical, of what *was* there – as the song has it, *you'll never miss your mother till she's buried beneath the clay.* For Belfast is changing daily: one day the massive Victorian façade of the Grand Central Hotel, latterly an army barracks, is *there*, dominating the whole of Royal Avenue; the next day it is gone, and a fresh breeze sweeps through the gap, from Black Mountain, across derelict terraces, hole-in-the-wall one-horse taxi operations, Portakabins, waste ground, to take the eye back up towards the mountain and the piled-up clouds.

The junk is sinking back into the sleech and muck. Pizza parlours, massage parlours, night-clubs, drinking-clubs, antique shops, designer studios momentarily populate the wilderness and the blitz sites; they too will vanish in the morning. Everything will be revised. The fly-specked gloom of The Elephant Bar is now a Winemark;

Mooney's Bar is a denim shop; The Gladstone has disappeared. The tangle of streets that was the Pound Loney is the Divis Flats Complex, which is also falling apart, its high-rise Sixties optimism sliding back into the rubble and erasure. Maps and street directories are suspect.

No, don't trust maps, for they avoid the moment: ramps, barricades, diversions, Peace Lines. Though if there is an ideal map, which shows this city as it is, it may exist in the eye of that helicopter ratcheting overhead, its searchlight fingering and scanning the micro-chip deviations: the surge of funerals and parades, swelling and accelerating, time-lapsed, sucked back into nothingness by the rewind button; the wired-up alleyways and entries; someone walking his dog when the façade of Gass's Bicycle Shop erupts in an avalanche of glass and metal forks and tubing, rubber, rat-trap pedals, toe-clips and repair kits. Or it may exist in photographs – this one, for example, of Raglan Street, showing

> . . . *a sight that was to become only too common to a generation of British soldiers as rioters stone 'A' Company, 2nd Battalion, The Queen's Regiment, during the savage Lower Falls riots of 3-5 July 1970 which left five civilians dead and eighteen military casualties . . .*

But the caption is inaccurate: the camera has caught only one rioter in the act, his stone a dark blip in the drizzly air. The others, these would-be or has-been or may-be rioters, have momentarily become spectators, as their protagonist does his David-and-Goliath act; some might be talking about the weather, which seems unusually grey for July, or maybe this is a bad print; some others are looking down Bosnia Street at what is happening or might happen next. The left-hand frame of the photograph only allows us the 'nia' of Roumania Street, so I don't know what's going on there, but I'm trying to remember – was I there that night, on this street littered with half-bricks, broken glass, a battered saucepan and a bucket? In this fragment of a map, here is the lamp-post where I swung as a child, there is Smyth's corner shop; I can almost see myself in the half-gloom and the din. From here – No. 100 – I would turn into Leeson Street, on up to the Falls Road, across to Clonard Street on my way to St Gall's Primary School; at least, that was how I was told to go, and generally I did, but remember, *Never go by Cupar Street*, my father would warn me, and I knew this was a necessary prohibition without asking why, for Cupar Street was one of those areas where the Falls and Shankill joined together as unhappy Siamese twins, one sporadically and mechanically beating the other round the head, where the Cullens, Finnegans and Reillys merged with Todds and Camerons and Wallaces. One day I did come home by Cupar Street, egged on by a fellow pupil. Nothing happened, and we felt the thrill of Indian scouts penetrating the British lines, the high of invisibility. We did it again; it became addictive, this perilous sin of disobedience and disappearance. We crept along in the dark shadow of the Falls Flax Spinning Mill, becoming bolder day by day in our deceit. For who knew what we were, who could tell? The forays ended when we were stopped one day by four boys about our own age. One of them had fashioned two little charity-type flags from paper and pins: he held a Union Jack in one hand, a tricolour in the other. He eyed us slyly, knowingly: *See them flags?* We nodded nervously. *Well, which of them would youse say was the best?* He had us cornered. If we chose the Union Jack, we were guilty of cowardice and treason – and he would know we were lying anyway; if we chose the tricolour, we would get a hiding. So we ran the gauntlet, escaping with a few bruises into the unspoken force-field of the Catholic end of the street. My father knew something was up when I got home; I broke down under questioning, and got a real hiding. I had learned some kind of lesson. So I thought.

I was reminded of this today, when I went out for what I imagined was a harmless spin on the bike. A showery day, blowing warm and cold – past the west side of Girdwood Barracks along Clifton Park Avenue – a few inhabited houses in a row of derelicts backing on to Crumlin Road Jail – up the Shankill; I come to the Shankill Road Library on the corner of Mountjoy Street (the name of yet another jail), remembering how I used to go here as a child in search of Biggles books because I had exhausted the entire Biggles stock of the Falls Library – I was older then, and was allowed to go, I think – how was it, across Cupar Street, up Sugarfield Street? I see the green cupola of Clonard Monastery towering high, almost directly above me, it seems, and I realise again with a familiar shock how little separates the Shankill and the Falls, how in the troubles of '68 or '69 it was rumoured that this monastery tower was a sniper's nest – so yes, I think, why not re-trace the route of all those years ago, 1959 or 1960. I turn idly down Mountjoy Street, Azamor Street, Sugarfield Street. Dead end. Here is the Peace Line, a thirty-foot-high wall scrawled with graffiti, mounted with drab corrugated iron; Centurion Street; Battenberg Street; dead end again. Where I remember rows of houses, factories, there is recent wasteland, broken bricks, chickweed, chain-link fencing. Eventually I find a new road I never knew existed – or is it an old street deprived of all its landmarks? – which leads into the Springfield Road. Familiar territory now, well, almost, for going down the Kashmir Road into Bombay Street –

burned out in '68, some new houses there – I come to the other side of the Peace Line, which now backs on to St Gall's School – still there, graffiticized, wire mesh on the windows, but still the same, almost; the massive granite bulk of Clonard is still there; Greenan's shop is now a dwelling; and the west side of Clonard Gardens, where the Flax & Rayon mill used to be, is all new houses; Charleton's shop is bricked up; Tolan's the barber's is long since gone, I knew that; this side of the street is all derelict, breeze-blocked, holes knocked into holes; so on to the Falls. I go down the road a bit, almost as far as the library, then stop; I'd like to go down the Grosvenor Road, so I make a U-turn and stop at the lights at the Grosvenor Road junction, and I'm just wondering what's the point, it's Sunday and there's no traffic about, and certainly no policemen, when somebody mutters something in my ear, I turn, and I'm grabbed round the neck by this character, while someone else has me by the arm, twisted up my back, another has the other arm and I'm hauled off the bike, *Right – where're you going? Here, get him up against the railings – what do you think you're at?* – Legs kicked apart, arms slapped up, *Right, here, get him here – come on, MOVE –* and I'm dragged across the road into what used to be McQuillan Street, only it isn't there any more, into one of these hole-in-the-wall taxi places, arms up against the breeze-block wall, legs apart, frisked, and all the time,

You were seen coming from the Shankill.
Why did you make a U-turn?
Who are you?
Where are you coming from?
Why did you stop when you seen the car?
You know the car.
The car. Outside Sinn Féin headquarters.

You looked at it.
You looked at it.
You were seen. You were seen.
Coming from the Shankill.
Where are you from?
Where is he from?
The Falls? When? What street?
What was the number of the house?
How far down the street was that?
When was that?
What streets could you see from the house?
Cape Street? Yeah.
Frere Street? Yeah. Where was Cape Street?
Again. Who lived next door?
Next door again.
Why did you stop when you seen the car?
Why did you turn?
So you moved up the road? When?
How old were you then?
Where was that? Mooreland?
Where is that?
Stockman's? Where is that?
What's next?
Casement? Right. What's next?
You were seen.
Where do you live now?
Where's that?
So where did you live again?
Yeah, I know it's not there any more.
You just tell me what was there.
Again. No. 100. Where was that?
You were seen.
What's the next street down from Raglan Street?
Coming from the Shankill . . . .

The questions are snapped at me like photographs.

The map is pieced together bit by bit. I am this map which they examine, checking it for error, hesitation, accuracy; a map which no longer refers to the present world, but to a history, these vanished streets; a map which is this moment, this interrogation, my replies. Eventually I pass the test. I am frisked again, this time in a regretful habitual gesture. *A dreadful mistake*, I hear one of them saying, *has been made*, and I get the feeling he is speaking in quotation marks, as if this is a bad police B-movie and he is mocking it, and me, and him.

I am released. I stumble across the road and look back; they have disappeared. I get on my bike, and turn, and go down the Falls, past vanished public houses – The Clock Bar, The Celtic, Daly's, The Gladstone, The Arkle, The Old House – past drapers, bakers, fishmongers, boot shops, chemists, pawnshops, picture houses, confectioners and churches, all swallowed in the maw of time and trouble, clearances; feeling shaky, nervous, remembering how a few moments ago I was *there*, in my mind's eye, one foot in the grave of that Falls Road of thirty years ago, inhaling its gritty smoggy air as I lolled outside the door of 100 Raglan Street, staring down through the comforting gloom to the soot-encrusted spires of St Peter's, or gazing at the blank brick gable walls of Balaklava Street, Cape Street, Frere Street, Milton Street, saying their names over to myself.

Punctuation

This frosty night is jittering with lines and angles, invisible
    trajectories:
Crackly, chalky diagrams in geometry, rubbed out the instant
    they're sketched,
But lingering in the head. The shots, the echoes, are like
    whips, and when you flinch,
You don't know where it's coming from. This bullet, is your
    name on it?
For the moment, everything is X, a blank not yet filled in.

Walking in the black space between the stars, I'm avoiding the
    cracks in the pavement.
And in the gap between the street-lights, my shadow seems
    to cross itself. I can
See my hand, a mile away in the future, just about to turn
    the latch-key in the lock,
When another shadow steps out from behind the hedge, going,
    dot, dot, dot, dot, dot . . . .

Yes

I'm drinking in the 7-Up bottle-green eyes of the barmaid
On the Enterprise express – bottles and glasses clinking each
    other –
When the train slows with a noise like Schweppes and halts
    just outside Dundalk.
Not that unwontedly, since we're no strangers to the border
    bomb.
As the Belfast accent of the tannoy tells us what is happening

I'm about to quote from Basho's *The Narrow Road to the Deep
    North* –
Blossoming mushroom: from some unknown tree a leaf has stuck to it –
When it goes off and we're thrown out of kilter. My mouth is
    full
Of broken glass and quinine as everything reverses South.

Revised Version

Trying to focus on the imagined grey area between Smithfield and North Street – jumbled bookstalls, fruitstalls, fleshers, the whingeing calls of glaziers and coal-brick men – I catch glimpses of what might have been, but it already blurs and fades; I wake or fall into another dream. I have before me Nesbitt's *The Changing Face of Belfast*, the first edition of 1968, and the second (revised) 1982 edition, which has somehow skimped on the ink, so that the dark threatening historicity of *High Street, looking east, 1851* – the stage-coach waiting, a one-legged man with a doomy placard tied to his back, two dogs fighting in the tramlines under the scratchy black clouds – has been replaced by a noon-day shimmer (we note the long morning shadows still) in which the dogs are merely playing, and the one-legged man proclaims salvation. We become aware of other shifts of emphasis, elisions and contractions, croppings: the observer taking a step backwards from *Victoria Square in the 1880s*, as if passing time has necessarily distanced the fixed past even more, and the new edition is a worn-out copy of the old; a photograph of The Ulster Institute for the Deaf and Dumb and Blind (1845-1963) becomes an old engraving of the same building; the entrance to Belfast Castle has vanished.

In waking life I expect streets which are not there. So, both versions of the *Demolition of Hercules Place, looking north, 1879* – one light, the other dark – suggest the ambivalence of this dilapidated present, the currency of time passing. For this could be now, 1987, as the Royal Avenue which the butchers' shambles of Hercules Place was to become is, in its turn, torn apart and a huge vista yawns through the vanished Grand Central Hotel (built to service a Central Railway Station that never was to be) to the Belfast Mountains, last refuge of the wolf and rebel. Transpose the dates: in 1879, two men in the right bottom corner have moved too quickly for the shutter; they are ghosts, wavering between memory and oblivion. Then a haze begins in the middle distance, the grainy dust of blitz sites and bad printing.

For everything is contingent and provisional; and the subjunctive mood of these images is tensed to the ifs and buts, the yeas and nays of Belfast's history. Going back another lifetime, to 1808, we find that *Mr Williamson proposes to make a new map of the town, but from the streets lately made, and the uncertain direction of others, it will be spring before any further progress will be made.* Spring became summer, autumn, winter; 'the map does not seem to have been produced'. It lives on in our imagination, this plan of might-have-beens, legislating for all the possibilities, guaranteed from censure by its non-existence. For maps cannot describe everything, or they describe states of mind, like Dubourdieu's 'very incorrect' *Plan of Belfast in 1811*, which shows *streets and blocks of buildings which have never existed; and also a bridge across the Lagan which was proposed but not carried out.* John Mulholland's Plan of 1788, dedicated to the Earl of Donegall, who owned half the town, shows a grand never-to-be canal flowing down the line of what was to be Chichester Street from the front of the White Linen Hall, now the City Hall, echoing the second Venice dreamed by George Macartney, Sovereign of Belfast in the late 1600s. Here too are 'intended streets', miasmas, projections on the reclaimed sleech which lies between the *ancient folded purple grits and shales of North Down and the tilted black basalts of Antrim, where on both sides of the river's mouth the valley sides fall back as if to form a great cup destined to hold the brimming city* – teetering and spilling, distilled from thin air, this intoxicating draught of futures swallowed at one gulp, as someone sets another up. We have seen Phillips' *New Cutt River* (on his Plan of 1685) before: not only does it almost follow the line of Mulholland's dream-canal, but it suggests the 1987 *Concept Plan for Laganside*, where a 'new cut' will make an island out of Maysfield, and the Blackstaff river is deculverted to form a marina; our architect has drawn little boats and happy figures here, absolving the stench and excrement and rubbish of the present. Here is the Eden of the future – gardens, fields, streams, clear water – looking like the banished past, before linen, ships, tobacco, ropes. We are going back to the source, as it is proposed that the Farset, which gave the town its name, be opened up again, this clear blue line leading up to the Albert Clock. Going back to Phillips, what are we to make of this *earthern rampart built in 1642, already partly obliterated at its north end*? Obliterated? Never finished? Proposed? And do we trust this *improvement made out on the strand*?

Improve, wipe out, begin again, imagine, change: the map appended to the Parliamentary Report of 1859 *shows very clearly the improvements effected by the making of Victoria Street and Corporation Street, which are laid down on the map over the old lanes and small streets, as follows*; so we follow the ghosts of Forest Lane, Weigh-House Lane, Back Lane, Elbow Lane, Blue Bell Entry, Stone Cutter's Entry, Quay Lane, Ireland's Entry, names that seem to spring up from an invented past. Or here, in 1853, we are shown *the Municipal Boundary of the Borough before its extension in 1853; after its extension; the Boundary of the Lighted and Watched Districts*, recalling the ordinance of 1680, that *Lights in Lanthorns be hunge at every other house doore or window time aboute in ye dark Nights from ye houres of six to tenn . . . to prevent disorders and mischeife*, later amended to *at their respective doores or shops one Lanthorne and candle lighted from ye houre of seaven oClock till ten at night when it is not moon-shine in ye saide houres* . . . .

As we shift sideways into the future of 30 August 1823, ignoring the *rival schemes to produce gas from the oil of Irish basking sharks*, we can clearly read a letter 60 yards distant from High Street's *extra large light in the form of a dolphin's head*; before we understand what it is telling us, or appreciate *the clear effulgence of a cloudless atmosphere illumined by the moon*, there is a whiff of ozone, a blue flicker, and we find ourselves stumbling through a ruinous Gasworks – midnight echo-chambers, clangorous retorts – as the 1300 miles of piping give up the ghost – a tiny whisper and a hiccup.

The maps are revised again, as a layer of toxic spoil would have to be removed from the whole site and the view across the Lagan from the Ormeau embankment completely transformed by the obliteration of the gasholders. The jargon sings of leisure purposes, velodromes and pleasure parks, the unfurling petals of the World Rose Convention. As the city consumes itself – scrap iron mouldering on the quays, black holes eating through the time-warp – the Parliamentary Under-Secretary of State for the Environment announces that *to people who have never been to Belfast their image of the place is often far-removed from the reality*. No more Belfast champagne, gas bubbled through milk; no more heads in ovens. Intoxication, death, will find their new connections. Cul-de-sacs and ring-roads. *The city is a map of the city.*

The Mouth

There was this head had this mouth he kept shooting off.
  Unfortunately.
It could have been worse for us than it was for him.
  Provisionally.
But since nothing in this world is certain and you don't know
  who hears what
We thought it was time he bit off more than he could chew.
  Literally.
By the time he is found there'll be nothing much left to tell
  who he was.

But of course some clever dick from the 'Forscenic Lab'
  reconstructs
Him, what he used to be – not from his actual teeth, not his
  fingerprints,
But from the core – the toothmarks of the first and last bite
  he'd taken of
This sour apple. But then we would have told them anyway.
  Publicity.

The Knee

His first bullet is a present, a mark of intelligence that will
End in the gutter behind The Clock Bar, since he keeps on
   doing what
He's not supposed to. The next one is for real, what we've
   just talked about.
It seems he was a hood, whatever, or the lads were just being
   careful.
Two and two were put together; what they added up to
   wasn't five.

Visiting time: he takes his thirteen-month-old son on his
   other knee.
Learning to walk, he suddenly throws himself into the
   staggering
Distance between his father and his father's father, hands
   held up high,
His legs like the hands of a clock, one trying to catch up on
   the other.

Brick

Belfast is built on *sleech* – alluvial or tidal muck – and is built *of* sleech, metamorphosed into brick, the city consuming its source as the brickfields themselves were built upon; sleech, this indeterminate slabbery semi-fluid – *all the public buildings*, notes Dr Pococke, visiting the town in 1752, *are founded on a morass* – this gunge, allied to *slick* and *sludge, slag, sleek* and *slush*, to the Belfast or Scots *sleekit* that means sneaky, underhand, not-to-be-relied-on, becoming, in the earnest *brick*, something definite, of proverbial solidity – *built like a brick shit-house*, we say; or, in dated slang, *you're a brick*. Yet even this paradigm of honesty has its verbal swamp. Its root is in *break*, related to the flaw in cloth known as a *brack*; worse, it is a cousin of *brock* – not the hardy badger, but rubbish, refuse, broken-down stuff, pig-swill, which is maybe why a German lager of that name never caught on in Northern Ireland. In anger, you might *come down like a ton of bricks* on someone; the victim might *shit a brick*. The subversive half-brick, conveniently hand-sized, is an essential ingredient of the ammunition known as 'Belfast confetti', and has been tried and trusted by generations of rioters; it is also known here as a *hicker* or a *heeker*, a word which seems to deal in the same currency as *hick, hack* and *howk*, pronounced *hoke* in these parts, meaning to dig or burrow; perhaps the defiant badger is in there somewhere after all, related to the superlative *wheeker*, which is another way of saying a *cracker*, something which is outstanding or *sticking out*.

Coal-brick – moulded from the brock of *slack* and coaldust – is here pronounced *breek*, reminding us of breeks, britches, bifurcations and alternatives, the breech of a gun. One of my abiding memories is the street-cry of the coal-brick man hawking his hand-cart through the smoggy backstreets, the bricks still steaming from the kiln – a long drawn-out *co-o-o-a-l br-e-e-e-k* ending in a glottal exclamation mark and mingling with the gulder of the brock-man or refuse-man, who bore with dignity and patience his occupational aroma of rotting tea-leaves and potato skins. Both were important links in the great chain of being which discarded nothing, the very building-blocks of matter recycled – milk-bottle tops, string, brown paper, rags; here I recall the rag-man's shed with its brick floor, mounds of old clothing, the musk of stale sweat. A world of cast-offs, hand-me-downs, of new lamps for old, realized in the incessant unravelling of my mother as woollen jumpers became scarves and socks and I held my arms at arm's length while she wound and wound. As the tall chimneys and the catacomb-like kilns of the brickworks crumbled back into the earth, the very city recycled itself and disassembled buildings – churches, air-raid shelters, haberdashers, pawnshops – were poured into the sleech of the lough shore to make new land; vast armies of binmen or waste-disposal experts laboured through the years transforming countless tons of brock into *terra firma*; the dredged-up sludge of the Lagan became Queen's Island, that emblem of solid work and Titanic endeavour.

Our new semi-detached house in Andersonstown – we moved there in 1955 – was built of *rustic* brick, an epithet I confused with *rusty*, for the material, rough-cast to mimic the weathered brick of rural cottages, seemed corroded,

73

pitted, burnt. It seemed a paradox that the house itself was new, smelling of bare plaster and wood-shavings. Behind us was about half an acre of not-yet-built-on land; not sleech, for we had forsaken the lowlands of the Lower Falls, but a truer clay, red, thick, heavy, satisfying, that could be moulded by hand. Through the clay there flowed a tiny stream surrounded by hawthorn hedges that were once a field division, where we built tree-houses and furtive shacks we believed invisible to adult eyes.

The stream itself had a magical secret quality, and I and my best friend Noel explored its banks in microscopic detail, performing evermore complex feats of miniature engineering in a series of dams, canals, harbours, breakwaters, run-offs, cul-de-sacs and overspills. We built and sank navies. We dug out fist-sized catacombs in its banks, under the clear water, and in them placed the corpses of birds, mice and frogs; months later we returned to them, probing, finding delicate clean skeletons. And from the clay itself we made towns and cities. These were guarded by bulwarks, ditches, palisades and outworks, for a necessary condition of the city was its eventual destruction; this was achieved by a catalogue of wars whose weapons were marbles, pebbles, or pellets moulded from clay – flicked by hand, since we considered catapults too brutal, the ultimate deterrent. These were elaborate sagas of advances, forays, skirmishes and truces, agreed-on interludes for repair or consolidation. My defences were always the first to go, the laying waste of my city a *fait accompli*. Noel's engineering was of a higher order. Where I would roll out sheets of clay and make slab walls, he would patiently make individual tiny bricks, building them up in such a way that if one brick was taken out, the structure would remain intact. His cities were fascist states; mine, a house of cards. My forts and palaces in ruins, we would join forces to destroy his stubborn battlements. I loved and admired him deeply, for his natural superiority extended to other domains: he was the fastest runner in the new estate; he had a peerless stamp collection; and he could fart at will. One day he asked me if I would like to be him. Perhaps he was asking if I loved him, or saying that he loved himself. At any rate, I said yes.

Some time later his family moved. I was devastated. I sulked around the house for weeks. The magical half-acre was now a patch of arid wasteland. The stream was a gutter.

Bit by bit, I made other friends; the intense detail came back, if only for a while. For the land we inhabited has long since been built over; the stream, the hawthorn hedges and the underwater cemetery are gone. Belfast has again swallowed up the miniature versions of itself in its intestine war.

The inevitable declension: *Brick.*
Brack.
Brock.

Apparition

The angelic old woman at the Friday morning second-hand
  market
Licks her finger and thumb and plucks little balls of fluff from
  off a jumper.
She smoothes out the wrinkles in a linen blouse and holds it to
  the light
And light shines through to meet the nearly-perfect sky-blue
  of her eye. Then
She dangles a 1940s pin-stripe suit at arm's length, as if
  measuring a corpse.

It reminds me of the character I met one night in The Hole-
  in-the-Wall Bar
Who was wearing a beat-up World War II flying-jacket
  frayed and split at the seams.
One arm was nearly hanging off. 'Just back from Dresden?',
  cracked the barman.
'Don't laugh', spat the character, 'my father was killed in this
  here fucking jacket.'

Night Out

Every Thursday night when we press the brass button on the
  galvanized wire mesh gate
A figure appears momentarily at the end of the strip-lit
  concrete passageway,
Then disappears. The gate squeaks open, slams shut almost
  instantly behind us.
Then through the semi-opaque heavy-duty polythene swing
  doors they might have taken
From a hospital. At the bar, we get the once-over once again.

Seven whiskeys later, the band is launching into *Four Green
  Fields*.
From somewhere out beyond the breeze-block walls we get a
  broken rhythm
Of machine-gun fire. A ragged chorus. So the sentence of the
  night
Is punctuated through and through by rounds of drink, of
  bullets, of applause.

Intelligence

We are all being watched through peep-holes, one-way mirrors, security cameras, talked about on walkie-talkies, car 'phones, Pye Pocketfones; and as this helicopter chainsaws overhead, I pull back the curtains down here in the terraces to watch its pencil-beam of light flick through the card-index – *I see the moon and the moon sees me*, this 30,000,000 candlepower gimbal-mounted Nitesun by which the operator can observe undetected, with his infra-red goggles and an IR filter on the light-source. Everyone is watching someone, everyone wants to know what's coming next, so the lightweight, transparent shield was a vast improvement over the earlier metal one because visibility was greatly increased and – an extra bonus – gave better protection against petrol and acid bombs which could flow through the grill mesh of the metal type . . . .

Or we note in passing that some walls in the city have been whitewashed to the level of a man's head so that patrolling soldiers at night are silhouetted clearly for snipers; or that one of these patrolling soldiers carries a Self-loading Rifle with an image intensification night-sight; that paint bombs are usually reserved for throwing at the vision blocks of APCs and armoured cars; and that passive observation is possible even on the darkest of nights, since the ambient light is amplified by this Telescope Starlight II LIEI 'Twiggy' Night Observation Device. Failing that, the 2B298 surveillance radar can identify moving man at 5,000 metres by the blips on its console. We track shadows, echoes, scents, prints; and in the interface the information is decoded, coded back again and stored in bits and bytes and indirect addressing; but the glitches and gremlins and bugs keep fouling-up, seething out from the hardware, the dense entangled circuitry of back streets, backplanes, while the tape is spooling and drooling over alphanumeric strings and random-riot situations; it seems the real-time clock is ticking away in the memory-dump, so look, let's get the relocating loader, since contrary to expectations water-cannon proved only marginally successful; few rioters seemed unduly convinced by a heavy soaking, especially in summer; better to use a random-access Monte Carlo method so that this clicking ticking Russian roulette will pay the house percentage, and we can then facilitate the provision of all manner of lighting devices, primarily to illuminate the removal of barriers which proliferated through the cities:

bread-vans, milk-carts, telegraph poles, paving-stones, lime trees, chestnuts, hawthorns, buses, tyres, fishing-lines, prams, JCBs, coal, shopping-trolleys, cement-mixers, lamp-posts, hoardings, people, sand, glass, breeze-blocks, corrugated iron, buckets, dustbins, municipal waste-bins, scaffolding, traffic signals, garden sheds, hedges, milk-churns, gas cylinders, chimney-pots, snow, oil-drums, gates, crazy paving, orange crates, fences, weighing-machines, earth, automatic chewing-gum dispensers, news-stands, camera tripods, ladders, taxis, dismantled football stadia, bicycles.

Keeping people out and keeping people in, we are prisoners or officers in Bentham's *Panopticon*, except sorting out who's who is a problem for the naïve user, and some compilers are inclined to choke on the mixed mode – panopticons within panopticons –

The Building circular – an iron cage, glazed – a glass lantern about the size of Ranelagh – The Prisoners in their Cells,

79

occupying the Circumference – The Officers (Governor, Chaplain, Surgeon, &c.), the Centre.

By Blinds, and other contrivances, the Inspectors concealed (except in so far as they think fit to show themselves) from the observation of the Prisoners: hence the sentiment of a sort of invisible omnipresence. – The whole circuit reviewable with little, or, if necessary, without any, change of place.

One station in the Inspection-Part affording the most perfect view of every Cell, and every part of every Cell, unless where a screen is thought fit occasionally and purposely to be interposed.

Against Fire (if, under a system of constant and universal inspection, any such accident could be apprehended), a pipe, terminating in a flexible hose, for bringing the water down into the central Inspection-Room, from a cistern, of a height sufficient to force it up again under its own pressure, on the mere turning of a cock, and spread it thus over any part within the Building.

For Visitors, at the time of Divine Service, an Annular Gallery, rising from a floor laid immediately on the ceiling of the Central Dome, the superior surface of which serves, after descent, for the reception of Ministers, Clerk, and a select part of the Auditory: the Prisoners all round, brought forward, within perfect view and hearing of the Ministers, to the front of their respective Cells.

Solitude, or limited Seclusion, ad libitum. *But, unless for punishment, limited seclusion in assorted companies is preferable: an arrangement, upon this plan alone, exempt from danger. The degree of Seclusion fixed upon this may be preserved, in all places, and at all times, inviolate. Hitherto, where solitude has been aimed at, some of its chief purposes have been frustrated by occasional associations.*

The Approach, one only – Gates opening into a walled avenue cut through the area. Hence, no strangers near the building without leave, nor without being surveyed from it as they pass, nor without being known to come on purpose. The gates, of open

*work, to expose hostile mobs: On the other side of the road, a wall
within a branch of the road behind, to shelter peaceable passen-
gers from the fire of the building.*

Hence the open chain-link fencing on the open routes
between areas of demarcation, the lazy swivelling eye of
the security camera; the invisibility of jails on maps, these
blank zones – on this 1986 reprint of the 1920 Ordnance
plan of North Belfast, for instance, where *the interesting
panopticon shape of the gaol is not shown here for security reasons*,
though it is *a sad reflection that apart from the one surviving
farm* (which, in any case, is now a barracks) *the only spaces
on this map are the prison exercise yard and the parade ground of the
military barracks* (which is half a barracks now, and half a
high-rise urban complex, only the prison remains in-
violate) – a sad reflection on what, on this ubiquitous
dense graffiti of public houses, churches, urinals, bonding
stores, graving docks, monuments, Sunday schools and
Orange halls – terraces and terraces of kitchen houses,
one-up-one-down houses, parlour houses, town houses,
back-to-back and front-to-back and back-to-front houses
– flour mills, swivel bridges, goods sheds, drinking
fountains, laundries, spinning mills, foundries, coffee
stalls, Gallaher's tobacco factory spewing smoke and snuff
and gouts of steam over railways, tramways, coal-quays,
and I see now through the time-warp something like the
Belfast of *Odd Man Out* as the camera pans down from
some aerial vision (the VTO craft pioneered by Shorts?)
into a mass of chimney stacks and mill-stacks churning
out this Titanic smoke over the spires and cupolas;
suddenly, I have just climbed the Whiterock Loney to
Black Mountain, and my father and I are sitting in the
Hatchet Field as he smokes a Gallaher's *Park Drive* and
points out, down in the inferno, Clonard Monastery, the

Falls Road, Leeson Street, the Clonard Picture-House, and the tiny blip of our house that we both pretend to see – down there, in the Beechmount brickfields, I can nearly see James Mason squatting in the catacomb of a brick kiln where I played Soldiers and Rebels, these derelict cloisters half-choked with broken brick and brick-dust, that are now gone, erased, levelled back into the clay, like all this brick-built demolition city, like this house we strain our eyes to see through the smog, homing in through the terraces and corner shops and spires and urinals to squat by the fire – coal-brick smouldering and hissing – while my father tells me a story . . . .

PART THREE

. . . people . . . in their daily walks continued
to follow streets that no longer existed,
but were only imaginary tracks through
a razed and empty section of Florence.

Kevin Lynch,
The Image of the City

I've just put on this
borrowed armour: second-hand
cold freezes my bones.

— Buson

Bed-Time Story

The sound effects were really very simple: a creaky leather wallet – here,
The speaker reached into his pocket and produced the very
    article –
Might stand for the marching boots of the Seven Dwarfs. Almost
    instantly,
I stepped into my father's creased, enormous shoes, their
    puckered insole ridges:
Cold, cold, so many hours until he comes back trudging
    through the snow,
The empty canvas sack around his neck; but never empty-
    handed – always promises
Of stories, or postcards left in limbo, *Not Known At This
    Address.* On the back,
You'll never guess who I met here – I'll tell you all about it when I see you.
Or bits of hairy twine come snaking out, the same gruff texture
As his navy-blue, tobacco-scented serge. The braid. The
    black mirror of his cap-peak.

And in the ink-dark celluloid, confused images of the narrative
    appear:
Disney's artists gather round like dwarfs, or ravens, as Disney
Flaps his arms to illustrate the story. He imitates a talking bird.
His hand opens and shuts like a beak. He gets them to do the
    same, to feel
The movement, the whole body swept along in mimicry, as
    they get it down
On paper. *He seemed to make it up as he went along.* Or maybe
    these were dreams,
Rehearsed for nights until they dawned into a blue
    configuration

Set off by floating, regal clouds; as if, already spoken-for and
    animated,
The day proclaimed its destination, knowing what was coming
    next. The way
A flock of birds will make a fist. Which flits open, shuts again,
    then vanishes.

For the blue is the sky of an air-mail letter, the clouds are puffs
    of smoke
Which punctuate my father's story. I see his fingernail is
    stained with nicotine,
Or maybe that's a trick of the light, the yellowish burnt umber
    which precedes
A thunderstorm. He is sprawled out on the sofa, I am in the
    rowing-boat
Between his knees. A squall will figure shortly, summoned-up
    from nowhere;
As this episode draws to a close, the castaway will cling to
    broken spars,
The tatters of his once-proud enterprise. By the island of
    tomorrow he will know
If he is drowned or saved; as yet, he's in the dark, treading
    amber water.
And now the time-lapsed, wind-torn envelope is swallowed in
    the cobalt night,
My father lies asleep; he's been abroad since early morning.

His hands are folded on his chest, as if fastened on a rosary.
He has gathered silence over him, like his overcoat I drape
    around me.
I feel its snowbound, dangling weight, the broad cuffs where
    my hands are lost,
The trailing hem. The regal crown of his cap. The cool damp
    head-band.

87

I touch the shining peak. Then the coarse weave of the sack.
   The glinting buckles.
I put on the leather harness. I step into the shoes again, and
   walk. I will deliver
Letters, cards, important gifts. I roll up a sleeve, and put my
   hand into his pocket.
His wallet. I open up its creaking leather palms, and I am rich:
I see myself in this, his photograph of me. He coughs, and stirs;
   his hands
Begin to sleepwalk, as if managing Pinocchio's wooden limbs.

In Kyoto, still
longing for Kyoto: cuck-
oo's two time-worn notes.

— Basho

Jawbox

What looks to us like a crackly newsreel, the picture
    jumping with flak,
Was clear as day, once. But that's taken as read, since this is a
    'quotation'
In the main text of the film, which begins with someone
    flicking open
The glossy pages of a *Homes and Gardens* kitchen supplement:
    Sink or Swim, the caption
Says, *The Belfast sink combines old-fashioned charm with tried and
    tested*
Practicality . . . 'Why *Belfast*?', the character begins to ponder –
    he puts the accent
On the *fast*, as if the name was Irish, which it was (or is); this
    is how
His father says it, just as, being from Belfast, he calls the
    sink a 'jawbox'.

At first you think the screen's gone blank, till you realise the
    camera
Has focussed on the sink itself: it has eaten up the whole
Picture. Then it backtracks, to reveal a Forties kitchen with a
    kind of wartime
Atmosphere: an old bakelite Clydesdale radio glows in the
    corner, humming
Over names like Moscow, Hilversum, Berlin. There's those
    jugs with blue and white
Striped bars, which give a premonition of the future (still
    our past) – filled
With flowers, they're déjà vu before their time, just as the
    sink, retired now

To the garden, overflows with hyacinths, geraniums.

There's something threatening about the kitchen – knives,
    glass, the epileptic
Buzzing of the overhead fluorescent strip, the white glaze
    blotched with calligraphic
Tea-leaves. Something in the pattern brings to mind an
    ornamental
Slightly murderous detail, and the picture changes with a
    click to show
The handcuffed metal *X*s of an old-style elevator gate.
    Someone's going down –
Chinese shadows flicking off and on across the various floors –
    to the Forensic Lab.
It's like suspicion, this weightless feeling in his stomach; and
    the clickety-clack
Reminds him of a railway journey, interrupted, for the
    seventh time that week,
By a bomb on the line between Dundalk and Newry. Or
    Newry and Dundalk, depending
Where you're coming from: like the difference between
    Cambodia and Kampuchea.

Shepherded on board an *Ulsterbus*, knowing now that the
    appointment won't be kept,
His attention wanders out across the rushy unkempt
    landscape, where a white dot
Concentrates his gaze. He lurches nearer. A hedge, a stone
    wall, gets in the way,
And then, brimming with water, wind-skimmed, rippled – he
    remembers how
He used to scoop an icy draught from it – the Belfast sink
    reveals itself.

91

It's now a cattle-trough, ripped out from a deconstructed
   farmhouse renovated
In the 'hacienda' style – not inappropriately, since *South of
   the Border*
Down Mexico Way is a big hit in these parts. Just then the border
   passes through him
Like a knife, invisibly, as the blip of the bus is captured on
   surveillance radar.

What's been stirring in his memory, like tea-leaves stirred in
   water –
He's elbow-deep in it, fingers trying to unblock the plug-hole
   – is the half-gnawed
Apple found at the *mise-en-scène*. The body, face-down on the
   steaming
Freshly-tarmacked road. He bites into the core, imagining
   his mouth's interior.
That twinge, an old occlusion. The tooth he broke on the rim of
   the jawbox
When he was eight. Blood-spattered white glaze; dilating, red
   confetti.
He spits out the pips and stares at the imaginary pith, seeing
   himself engraved there:
Furrows, indentations, grooves, as crisp as fingerprints. A
   little hinge of skin.

The mouth suggests the body –
Biting, grinding, breathing, chewing, spitting, tasting;
   clenched
In a grimace or a smile – his child's body, hunched in the dark
   alcove underneath
The sink, sulking, tearful, wishing he was dead. Imprisoned
   by so many

Small transgressions, he wants to break out of the trap. He's
    caught between
Bel*fast* and *Bel*fast, in the accordion pleats between two
    lurching carriages
Banging, rattling, threatening to break loose, as he gets a
    terrifying glimpse
Of railway sleepers, blotchy gravel flicking past a smell of
    creosote and oil and urine.

The coupling snaps; another mouth floats into view, its rust-
    tinged canine edges
Sealed in labelled see-through polythene; there's an *O* of
    condensation. From the cloud
A face begins to dawn: something like his own, but thicker,
    coarser, Jekyll
Turning into Hyde – an Englishman into an Irishman –
    emerging from the bloom
Behind the mirror. Breathed-on, becoming whole, the
    murderer is hunched
Behind the hedge. One bite from the apple, as the victim's
    Ford Fiesta trickles
Up the driveway. The car door opens. The apple's thrown
    away.

There's a breath of fresh tar. The scent will always summon
    up that afternoon,
As it blossoms into apple, into mouth. It's hanging in the air
    as Dr Jekyll finally
Makes it into Belfast. Beyond the steamed-up window, the half-
    dismantled gasworks
Loom up, like a rusty *film noir* laboratory – carboys, vats,
    alembics, coils, retorts.
It's that effect where one image warps into the other, like the
    double helix

93

Of the DNA code, his footsteps dogged throughout the action
    by another. Or
A split screen might suggest the parallels of past and present,
    Jekyll ticking
Downwards in the lift, as Hyde runs down the spiral stairwell.
    Till they meet.

What looks to us like a crackly newsreel, the picture jumping
    with flak,
Is the spotted, rust-tinged mirror screwed above the Belfast
    sink. Jekyll's head
Is jerking back and forward on the rim. Red confetti spatters
    the white glaze.
The camera backtracks to take in a tattered *Homes and
    Gardens* kitchen supplement.
A pair of hands – *lean, corded, knuckly, of a dusky pallor, and
    thickly shadowed*
With swart hair – come into view, and flick the pages of the
    magazine.
Bel*fast*, the voice says, not *Bel*fast. Then the credits roll.

Darkness never flows
except down by the river:
shimmering fireflies.

— Chiyo

John Ruskin in Belfast

As I approached the city, the storm-cloud of the Nineteenth
    Century
Began to wheel and mass its pendulous decades; the years
    grew weighty, slate-grey,
Palpable, muttering with dark caesurae, rolling in a clattering
    mockery
Of railway-luggage trains. All this while, the minutes seethed
    forth as artillery-smoke
Threatening to collapse into a dank fog. A single gauzy patch
    of iris blue –
All that remained of the free azure – contracted, shrank into
    oblivion
Till it became all pupil, olive-black, impenetrable; jagged
    migraine lightning
Flashed in the dark crock of my brain.

Like Turner, lashed to the mast of the *Ariel*, the better to see
    what he later painted –
The unwearied rage of memory, no distinction left between the
    sea and air –
I am riding out the hurricane, the writhing cloudscape of the
    sea collapsing
Into masses of accumulated yeast, which hang in ropes and
    wreaths from wave to wave;
Gouts and cataracts of foam pour from the smoky masts of the
    industrial Armada
As the wrack resolves itself in skeins and hanks, in terraces
    and sinks and troughs;
The air is sick with vitriol, the hospital-sweet scent of snuff,
    tobacco, linen.

And the labyrinthine alleyways are bloody with discarded
    bandages, every kind of ordure:
The dung of horses, dogs and rats and men; the knitted,
    knotted streets
Are crammed with old shoes, ashes, rags, smashed crockery,
    bullet casings, shreds
Of nameless clothes, rotten timber jaggy with bent nails,
    cinders, bones and half-bricks,
Broken bottles; and kneaded into, trampled, or heaving,
    fluttering, dancing
Over all of these, the tattered remnants of the news, every kind
    of foul advertisement,
The banner headlines that proclaim an oceanic riot, mutilated
    politics,
The seething yeast of anarchy: the very image of a pit, where a
    chained dwarf
Savages a chained bulldog.

As I strove against this lethargy and trance within myself,
    dismembered
Fragments of my speech, *The Mystery of Life and Its Arts*, swam
    up through the cumulus:
This strange agony of desire for justice is often, I think, seen in
    Ireland –
For being generous-hearted, and intending always to do right, you
    still neglect
External laws of right, and therefore you do wrong, without conceiving
    of it;
And so fly into wrath when thwarted, and will not admit the possibility
    of error . . . .
See how in the static mode of ancient Irish art, the missal-painter draws
    his angel
With no sense of failure, as a child might draw an angel, putting red
    dots

In the palm of each hand, while the eyes – the eyes are perfect circles, and,
I regret to say, the mouth is left out altogether.

That blank mouth, like the memory of a disappointed smile,
    comes back to haunt me.
That calm terror, closed against the smog and murk of Belfast:
    Let it not open
That it might condemn me. Let it remain inviolate.
Or let that missing mouth be mine, as, one evening in Siena
I walked the hills above, where fireflies moved like finely-
    broken starlight
Through the purple leaves, rising, falling, as the cobalt
    clouds – white-edged, mountainous –
Surged into thunderous night; and fireflies gusted everywhere,
    mixed with the lightning,
Till I thought I'd open up my mouth and swallow them, as I
    might gulp the Milky Way.

When the last star fades into the absolute azure, I will return
To where *The Dawn of Christianity*, by Turner, hangs in
    Belfast in its gilt frame:
Airy, half-discovered shades of aqua, the night becoming hazy
    milk and pearl,
The canvas is a perfect circle; and as I gaze into its opalescent
    mirror
I try to find its subject, *The Flight into Egypt*. A palm tree
    beckons
Like an angel's hand: words issue from the sealed tomb of his
    mouth – *Be thou there*
Until I bring thee word – and the Holy Family vanishes into the
    breathed-on mirror
Where the Nile-blue sky becomes the Nile, abandoning the
    Empire
To its Massacre of Innocents, the mutilated hands and knees
    of children.

Eleven horsemen –
not one of them turns his head –
through the wind-blown snow.

— Shiki

Narrative in Black and White

Now take these golf balls, scattered all around the place,
   which since
The reproduction's blurred, you'd easily misconstrue as
   ping-pong –
You can't make out the dimples. But they're different as
   chalk and cheese:
Ever get hit by a golf ball? You'd know all about it. And
   perhaps
The golf club in the bottom corner is no give-away. People
   have been known
To mistake it for a gun. And the disembodied plus-fours
Might be army surplus. No, all these things are dangerous
   enough,
According to whose rules you play. Which is maybe why
   they're put there,
Where you'd least expect them, floating against the
   façade of the Europa.

Hotel, that is. You know it? Looks as if it's taken from a
   photograph,
Down to the missing *E* of the logo, the broken windows,
   which they only got
Around to fixing last week. Things drift off like that, or
   people drift in.
Like Treacy, who it's all about, according to the guy who
   painted it.

This splash of red here: not blood, but a port-wine stain or
    strawberry mark
That Treacy carried all his life, just here, above the wrist-
    watch. Any time
You saw him sitting, he would have his right hand over it. Like
    this.
Too easily recognised, he didn't like. This is where the black
    gloves
Come in, gripping the revolving foyer doors. Or maybe one
    of them
Is raised, like saying *Power* – to the people, to himself, whatever.

Billiard balls? Well, maybe. Certainly these random scratches
    on the canvas
Suggest the chalk-marks on a green baize, a faded diagram
    from which
You'd try to piece together what the action was. Like trying
    to account
For Treacy's movements. Though on the night in question,
    according to the barman
In The Beaten Docket, he'd staggered in from some win on
    the horses,
Slaps a tenner on the counter, and orders a 'Blue Angel'. Blue
    what?
Says the barman. Angel, Treacy says, Blue Bols, vodka, ice,
    a drop of sugar.
Oh, and top it up with whipped cream. I say this just to show
    the sort
Of him, like someone who a year or two ago would not have
    known cocktail
From a hen's arse. You're sure, the barman says, you
    wouldn't like a straw?

The staircase is important. The zig-zag is like taking one step forward,

Two steps back. For who would take the stairs up thirteen floors, when

He could take the lift? The reason why, the power had gone that night.

So only one way in, and one way out. As sure as meeting your own shadow.

This, I think, is what the mirror represents. Like, everybody knew about the split,

And what side Treacy ended up on. Of course, the detail's lost;

You have to see it like it is, original. The colours, the dimensions.

Even the frame, like someone spying through binoculars, is saying something:

I'm watching you; but you, you can't see me. Ping-pong. Yin-yang.

So here is Treacy, at the wrong end of the telescope, diminishing.

He was seen in this bar, that bar. Like what I'm saying is, that anybody

Might have fingered him. So the man on the thirteenth floor sits pat.

He draws back the curtain. He stares through the kaleidoscope of snow

And sees what's coming next. Treacy's footsteps. Game, set and match.

They found him in the empty room. The face was blown off. They rolled down

One black glove. A Rorschach blot. The Red Hand, as he called himself.

Me? I knew him like a brother. Once. But then our lives grew
    parallel, if
Parallel is never meeting. He started dressing up and talking
    down. What
He would and wouldn't do. And people don't go shooting off
    their mouths like that.

Wild rough seas tonight:
yawning over Sado Isle,
snowy galaxies.

— Basho

Hamlet

As usual, the clock in The Clock Bar was a good few minutes
　　fast:
A fiction no one really bothered to maintain, unlike the story
The comrade on my left was telling, which no one knew for
　　certain truth:
Back in 1922, a sergeant, I forget his name, was shot outside the
　　National Bank . . . .
Ah yes, what year was it that they knocked it down? Yet, its
　　memory's as fresh
As the inky smell of new pound notes – which interferes with
　　the beer-and-whiskey
Tang of now, like two dogs meeting in the revolutionary 69 of
　　a long sniff,
Or cattle jostling shit-stained flanks in the Pound. For *pound*, as
　　some wag
Interrupted, was an off-shoot of the Falls, from the Irish, *fál*,
　　a hedge;
Hence, *any kind of enclosed thing*, its twigs and branches
　　commemorated
By the soldiers' drab and olive camouflage, as they try to melt
Into a brick wall; red coats might be better, after all. *At any rate,*
This sergeant's number came up; not a winning one. The bullet had
　　his name on it.
Though Sergeant X, as we'll call him, doesn't really feature
　　in the story:
The nub of it is, *This tin can which was heard that night,*
　　trundling down
From the bank, down Balaklava Street. Which thousands heard, and
　　no one ever

105

Saw. Which was heard for years, any night that trouble might be
Round the corner . . . and when it skittered to a halt, you knew
That someone else had snuffed it: a name drifting like an
 afterthought,
A scribbled wisp of smoke you try and grasp, as it becomes
 diminuendo, then
Vanishes. For *fál*, is also *frontier*, *boundary*, as in *the undiscovered*
 country
From whose bourne no traveller returns, the illegible, thorny hedge
 of time itself –
Heartstopping moments, measured not by the pulse of a wrist-
 watch, nor
The archaic anarchists' alarm-clock, but a mercury tilt device
Which 'only connects' on any given bump on the road. So, by
 this wingèd messenger
The promise 'to pay the bearer' is fulfilled:

As someone buys another round, an Allied Irish Banks £10
 note drowns in
The slops of the counter; a Guinness stain blooms on the
 artist's impression
Of the sinking of *The Girona*; a tiny foam hisses round the
 salamander brooch
Dredged up to show how love and money endure, beyond
 death and the Armada,
Like the bomb-disposal expert in his suit of salamander-cloth.
Shielded against the blast of time by a strangely-mediaeval
 visor,
He's been outmoded by this jerky robot whose various
 attachments include
A large hook for turning over corpses that may be booby-trapped;
But I still have this picture of his hands held up to avert the
 future

In a final act of *No surrender*, as, twisting through the murky fathoms
Of what might have been, he is washed ashore as pearl and coral.

This *strange eruption to our state* is seen in other versions of the Falls:
A no-go area, a ghetto, a demolition zone. For the ghost, as it turns out –
All this according to your man, and I can well believe it – this tin ghost,
Since the streets it haunted were abolished, was never heard again.
The sleeve of Raglan Street has been unravelled; the helmet of Balaklava
Is torn away from the mouth. The dim glow of Garnet has gone out,
And with it, all but the memory of where I lived. I, too, heard the ghost:
A roulette trickle, or the hesitant annunciation of a downpour, ricocheting
Off the window; a goods train shunting distantly into a siding,
Then groaning to a halt; the rainy cries of children after dusk.
For the voice from the grave reverberates in others' mouths, as the sails
Of the whitethorn hedge swell up in a little breeze, and tremble
Like the spiral blossom of Andromeda: so suddenly are shrouds and branches
Hung with street-lights, celebrating all that's lost, as fields are reclaimed
By the Starry Plough. So we name the constellations, to put a shape
On what was there; so, the storyteller picks his way between the isolated stars.

But, *Was it really like that?* And, *Is the story true?*
You might as well tear off the iron mask, and find that no one, after all,
Is there: nothing but a cry, a summons, clanking out from the smoke
Of demolition. Like some son looking for his father, or the father for his son,
We try to piece together the exploded fragments. Let these broken spars
Stand for the Armada and its proud full sails, for even if
The clock is put to rights, everyone will still believe it's fast:
The barman's shouts of *time* will be ignored in any case, since time
Is conversation; it is the hedge that flits incessantly into the present,
As words blossom from the speakers' mouths, and the flotilla returns to harbour,
Long after hours.